Approaching
according to the Athri Cycle

Oral Teachings by
Kyabje Menri Tridzin Lungtog Tenpai Nyima Rinpoche
given in conjunction with Sherab Jamma Empowerment,
Shenten Dargye Ling, France, August 26 – 28, 2010

Orally translated, transcribed, compiled and edited by
Khenpo Tenpa Yungdrung, Carol Ermakova and Dmitry Ermakov

Public Series A

FOUNDATION FOR
THE PRESERVATION
OF YUNGDRUNG BÖN
WWW.YUNGDRUNGBON.CO.UK

Published by
Foundation for the Preservation of Yungdrung Bön

Copyright © Kyabje Lungtog Tenpai Nyima, Khenpo Tenpa Yungdrung,
Dmitry Ermakov, Carol Ermakova, 2016

Cover art and book layout © Dmitry Ermakov, 2016

Title page and back cover photos courtesy Rosa-Maria Mendez.
Photo on p. 2 courtesy of Yongdzin Lopön Tenzin Namdak.
Images on pp. 13 & 15 courtesy of Christophe Moulin.

Footnotes, Tibetan terms, Bibliography & Suggested Reading by Dmitry Ermakov.

ISBN: 978-0-9955368-0-7

**FOUNDATION FOR
THE PRESERVATION
OF YUNGDRUNG BÖN**
WWW.YUNGDRUNGBON.CO.UK

FPYB is a charitable non-profit
organization. All proceeds from
sales are reinvested into ongoing
projects.

Dedicated to the Long-Life of
Kyabje Menri Tridzin Lungtog Tenpai Nyima Rinpoche and
to continued spread of authentic Yungdrung Bön in the world.

Preface

Six years have passed since Kyabje Menri Tridzin Lungtog Tenpai Nyima Rinpoche's visit to Shenten Dargye Ling Bönpo Centre in Blou, France, at the end of August 2010. During the visit, Rinpoche gave wonderfully detailed and lucid instructions on the Preliminary Practices and an Introduction to Dzogchen according to the Athri Dzogchen Cycle. After three days of teachings, he bestowed the empowerment of Sherab Jamma, The Wisdom Goddess of Loving-Kindness, a powerful finale for this auspicious occasion.

Carol and I were tasked with producing the edited transcript of these teachings. This, however, presented certain challenges since Kyabje Menri Tridzin Rinpoche taught in Tibetan. His discourse was simultaneously and ably interpreted by Dr. Stéphane Arguillère with interjections and commentaries by Khenpo Tenpa Yungdrung. The initial transcript was a patchwork of repetitions and double takes, requiring significant re-ordering and editing, all the more so since this was intended for public publication.

Khenpo Tenpa Yungdrung, Carol and I set about checking the text the following month. It soon became apparent there was still much work to be done, and we had to go back to the original audio tapes to finalize several difficult passages. As we listened, Khenpo Tenpa Yungdrung retranslated them orally and we then rearranged the resulting material into a more concise order. Without Khenpo's input this book would never have come about, so we would like to thank him for his efforts, enthusiasm and dedication.

By the end of our work sessions in September 2010, the text was starting to take shape, but it still required extensive editing, both linguistic and structural, as well as additional references, footnotes and transliteration of Bönpo terms. Here I would like to thank Dr. Sangmo Yangri for sending me relevant Tibetan books from the Central Institute of Higher Tibetan Studies, Sarnath, Varanasi, India, without which proper referencing would not have been possible.

Since Carol and I are extremely busy with producing a large number of transcripts, translations, public books and multi-media materials on Bön, often working on several projects at the same time, the process of bringing this publication to completion has taken several years. The final revision and editing was completed in August 2016 and we are both happy to present this volume to the readers.

Kyabje Menri Tridzin Rinpoche's unique teaching style combines scholastic brilliance and profound experiential instructions with humour and knowledge of realities of life. This book will be equally useful to all, from those who have just discovered the Yungdrung Bön tradition to academicians and scholars, students as well as, of course, practitioners.

We wish and pray that this book will bring benefit to all who meet with it!

Mustsug Marro!

རྒྱ་ཚོ་རྒྱ་རྒྱ་རྫོགས་པ་སྨྲ་ལ་རོཏ༔

Dmitry Ermakov,
North Pennines, UK,
14 August 2016

~ ii ~

Biography of Kyabje Menri Tridzin Rinpoche

Kyabje Menri Tridzin Lungtog Tenpai Nyima Rinpoche[1] is the 33rd Abbot of Menri Monastery and the Supreme Head of the Yungdrung Bön[2] tradition. He was born in Amdo[3] province of Tibet in 1927 and became a monk at the age of eight in Kyangtsang Monastery.[4] At sixteen, he entered the Dialectic School there and obtained his *geshe*[5] degree at twenty-four. At the age of twenty-six, he travelled to Gyalrong[6] from where he brought a copy of *Kangyur*[7] back to his monastery. He then departed to Tsang where he continued his studies at Yungdrung Ling, Menri and Kharna[8] Bönpo monasteries, after which he went to Drepung[9] Gelugpa[10] monastery in Lhasa[11] where he

---

[1] Tib, Skyab rje Sman ri Khri 'dzin Lung rtogs Bstan pa'i nyi ma Rin po che / སྐྱབ་རྗེ་ སྨན་རི་ཁྲི་འཛིན་བསྟན་པའི་ཉི་མ་རིན་པོ་ཆེ།

[2] Tib. G.yung drung bon / གཡུང་དྲུང་བོན།

[3] Tib . A mdo / ཨ་མདོ།

[4] Tib. Kyang tsang dgon / སྐྱང་ཚང་དགོན།

[5] Tib. dge bshe / དགེ་བཤེ།

[6] Tib. Rgyal rong / རྒྱལ་རོང་།

[7] Tib. bka' 'gyur / བཀའ་འགྱུར།

[8] Tib. G.yung drung gling, Bkra shis Sman ri gling, Mkhar sna Bsam gtan gling / གཡུང་དྲུང་གླིང་། བཀྲ་ཤིས་སྨན་རི་གླིང་། མཁར་སྣ་བསམ་གཏན་གླིང་།

[9] Tib. 'Bras spungs / འབྲས་སྤུངས།

[10] Tib. Dge lugs pa / དགེ་ལུགས་པ།

[11] Tib. Lha sa / ལྷ་ས།

stayed until the Tibetan uprising in 1959. At that time, he fled on foot to Mustang, then proceeded to Pokhara and on to India.

He later joined Sherab Tenpai Gyaltsen Rinpoche,[12] the Abbot of Yungdrung Ling, who had also managed to escape the hostilities, and other important Bönpo lamas in Samling[13] monastery in Dolpo, Nepal. which contained a large collection of Bönpo manuscripts. Since any precious Bönpo texts were destroyed as result of Chinese takeover of Tibet, the extensive collection of manuscripts held at Samling proved invaluable. Geshe Sanggye Tenzin Jongdong,[14] as he was then called, reprinted them in India together with Lopön Tenzin Namdak and other scholars.

At Samling he also met Dr. David Snellgrove from SOAS, University of London, who invited him to England as a research assistant along with Lopön Tenzin Namdak[15] and Geshe Samten Gyaltsen Karmay.[16] During his time in the West, Geshe Sanggye Tendzin Jongdong taught Tibetan culture and religion alongside studying Western culture and spirituality. He stayed at stayed Christian monasteries of various catholic orders and visited the Pope Paul II in Rome.

In 1964, he returned to India and was sent by H.H. Dalai Lama as Head Master to a school in Mussoorie where he stayed for three years. In 1965, Lopön Tenzin Namdak purchased land in Dolanji, Himachal Pradesh, with the help of the Catholic Relief Service, which became the site of the settlement for the Tibetan Bönpo community in exile. In 1968, during a week-long series of rituals and divinations

---

[12] Tib. Shes rab bstan pa'i rgyal mtshan Rin po che / ཤེས་རབ་བསྟན་པའི་རྒྱལ་མཚན་རིན་ པོ་ཆེ།

[13] Tib. Bsam gling dgon pa / བསམ་གླིང་དགོན་པ།

[14] Tib. Sangs rgyas bstan 'dzin ljong ldong / སངས་རྒྱས་བསྟན་འཛིན་ལྗོང་ལྡོང་།

[15] Tib. Slob dpon Bstan 'dzin rnam dag / སློབ་དཔོན་བསྟན་འཛིན་རྣམ་དག

[16] Tib. Dge bshes Bsam gtan rgyal mtshan Mkhar rme'u / དགེ་བཤེས་བསམ་གཏན་རྒྱལ་ མཚན་མཁར་རྨེའུ།

performed at the Dolanji settlement by the most senior Bönpo lamas, Geshe Sanggye Tendzin Jongdong was selected by the Protectors of Bön to become the 33rd Holder of the Throne of Menri Monastery and the Supreme Head of Yungdrung Bön. At that time, Menri Tridzin Rinpoche was in Oslo, Norway, at the invitation of Prof. Per Kvaerne. Upon receiving a telegram from India with news of his new appointment, he promptly returned to Dolanji and assumed his duty, along with the name Kyabje Menri Tridzin Lungtog Tenpai Nyima Rinpoche.

Since then, he has been working tirelessly to re-establish and preserve the Yungdrung Bön tradition both in exile and Tibet. He has personally overseen the construction and development of Menri Monastery in exile, Bön Children's Home, Bön Children's Welfare Centre, Central School for Tibetans and Redna Menling[17] Bönpo Nunnery in Dolanji. In recent years, Menri Tridzin Rinpoche has frequently travelled in the West where he has given numerous teachings and empowerment.

---

[17] Tib. Rad na sman gling / རད་ན་སྨན་གླིང་།

Approaching Dzogchen
according to the Athri Cycle

Modern history of Yungdrung Bön

First of all, I would like to say a few words about the general situation [of Yungdrung Bön in recent decades].

Yongdzin Tenzin Namdak Rinpoche was already the Yongdzin – "teacher of teachers" – in the Menri monastery of Tibet before the Chinese invasion. He later went to India, as did the abbot of Yungdrung Ling monastery, and the previous Yongdzin Rinpoche, Sanggye Tenzin.[18] Thus they were able to re-establish the Bön teachings in exile. I will not retell the story of how they left Tibet; much could be told, but that is in the past now. Instead, I will explain a little bit about how the Bön tradition was re-established in India. There were two main monastic seats, that of Menri and that of Yungdrung Ling, and the senior lamas of both were able to escape. In exile, they collaborated to ensure the Bön tradition would be preserved.

Soon after arriving in India, Yongdzin Rinpoche, myself and Geshe Samten Karmay were invited to England by Professor Snellgrove. In fact, twenty-four scholarly Tibetans went abroad with the blessing of H.H. XIV Dalai Lama and were scattered in groups of two or three in universities in the West. The three Bönpo scholars

---

[18] Tib. Yongs 'dzin Slob dpon Sangs rgyas bstan 'dzin Rin po che / ཡོངས་འཛིན་སློབ་ དཔོན་སངས་རྒྱས་བསྟན་འཛིན་རིན་པོ་ཆེ།

were based in London for three years, and during that time we thought over how we should best proceed to preserve our tradition.

Upon returning to India, Yongdzin Rinpoche was called for an audience with H.H. XIV Dalai Lama, who stressed that while he himself would do all he could to support Bönpos in exile, the main responsibility lay with Yongdzin Rinpoche. He went on to say that unfortunately, as there were relatively few Bönpos in India at the time, he would not be able to secure land for us. If, however, we were able to acquire land ourselves, he would support this. So we had to find a way to acquire land by ourselves, a place where we could work to restore our traditions ourselves. In this way, with the help of the Swiss Red Cross, a Bönpo settlement was established in Dhorpatan, Nepal. Later, with the help of the Catholic Relief Service, Yongdzin Rinpoche was able to buy land for a settlement in Dolanji, India. At that time, I was sent as a school teacher by the Dalai Lama to Mussoorie. The lamas who had come from Tibet settled there and were able to re-establish the Menri monastery there. It was here that the two Yongdzins – Sanggye Tenzin Rinpoche and Tenzin Namdak Rinpoche – taught and resided. As you all know, a second monastery was established later: Triten Norbutse,[19] in Nepal.

Fig. 1 Yongdzin Lopön Sanggye Tenzin and Yongdzin Lopön Tenzin Namdak in India. Courtesy of YLTNR.

---

[19] Tib. Khri brtan nor bu'i rtse / ཁྲི་བརྟན་ནོར་བུ་ཚེ།

When we use the term 'monastery' or '*gompa*'[20] this implies monastic life. Nowadays we see all kinds of institutes and teaching centres all over the world but a monastery is quite different. The root is the same, but there is a difference. What is the difference?

Monastic life is based on *vinaya*,[21] the monastic rules, while in a teaching centre or institute all sorts of people can come and receive teachings on Sutra, Tantra or Dzogchen. Monks must keep their rules and vows purely and remain within the boundary of the monastery. There are many other types of practitioner, such as *ngagpas*,[22] lay yogis, yoginis and so on.

The main focus or aim in both Menri Monastery and Triten Norbutse Monastery is to provide the monks with a full training in dialectics so that they can obtain the *geshe* degree. There are many subjects to study, from Sutra, Tantra or Dzogchen, but these are included in the *geshe* curriculum, and this is the foundation for later becoming a *khenpo*[23] or *lopön*; one cannot become a *lopön* or *khenpo* without first being a *geshe*.

So although the Bönpos were few in number, we decided to focus our efforts on the teachings. Moreover, the Bönpos came from many different regions of Tibet, such as Kham, Amdo and Utsang,[24] and the families and lamas from the various regions wanted to stay together. In particular, there were very few older lamas, and they were passing away one after the other; there are only Yongdzin Rinpoche and myself left of the older generation. The middle generation is also all but non-existent – there are no lamas in their fifties, sixties or seventies. Look around you, our *geshes* here are all under fifty.

---

[20] Tib. dgon pa / དགོན་པ།

[21] Tib. 'dul ba / འདུལ་བ།

[22] Tib. sngags pa / སྔགས་པ།

[23] Tib. mkhan po / མཁན་པོ།

[24] Tib. Khams, A mdo, Dbu gtsang / ཁམས། ཨ་མདོ། དབུ་གཙང་།

Nevertheless, even in this younger generation there are over a hundred monks who have already passed their *geshe* degree from Menri Monastery or Triten Norbutse. Now connections with Tibet are good so there are many monks who come from Tibet to study in India or Nepal, and several *geshes* have been able to go back to Tibet to teach what they have learned. They have also spread out in other parts of India and the West, so we have a very good foundation.

Before we three Bönpo scholars went to England, and then later travelled in Europe and America, some Western scholars had written books about Bön, but actually, they had no clue about it. The closest some of them went was to the border, to places such as Kalimpong, where they asked questions: 'So what is this so-called Bön?' and then they wrote books based on the stories they were told. Professor Snellgrove, however, conferred with we three fully-trained Bönpo lamas to translate a Bön text, and it is thanks to him that the first serious book was published in the West. This book is *The Nine Ways of Bon*.[25]

Now we have many *geshes* and many of them are teaching. For example, there is the Ligmincha Institute in America which is very good, but now it is my great aspiration and wish that Bön might be well established here in Europe thanks to the teachings of Yongdzin Rinpoche and Khenpo Rinpoche. You have to help them develop this place. This must become a centre for Dzogchen. In fact, the source of Dzogchen teachings comes from the Bön tradition, but people don't acknowledge this, saying there is no Dzogchen in Bön. So it is your duty now to prove, through your practice and study, whether Bön has Dzogchen or not.

---

[25] Snellgrove, David. *The Nine Ways of Bön*, (London: Oxford University Press, 1967).

The historical origins of Yungdrung Bön

H.H. XIV Dalai Lama has acknowledged the value of Bön saying that the native religion, the native culture of Tibet, is Bön. Otherwise, many historians have said that there was nothing in Tibet – no culture, no literature or writing system – during the reigns of the thirty-three kings before Srongtsen Gampo.[26] They say that during this time Tibet was completely barbaric and uncivilized. If they mention Bön, it is in the context of primitive, 'shamanic' rituals. Now, since his H. H. the Dalai Lama has recognized Bön as the native religion of Tibet, more and more people are becoming aware of the Bön tradition.

In Varanasi there is an institute in Sarnath called the Central Institute of Higher Tibetan Studies, where there were originally four sections: Nyingma, Kagyud, Sakya[27] and Gelug, and now there is also a fifth, a Bönpo section. A lot of research has been done there and this has resulted in the publication of a large book which establishes that Dzogchen is actually originally something Tibetan. It did not come from India. There is no single word of Dzogchen in the Gelug tradition, nor in the Sakya or Kagyud. In the Nyingma, they accept Dzogchen as well as the Thegpa Rimgu,[28] the theory of the Nine Vehicles or Ways. But basically, according to this theory, it can be established that Dzogchen did not come from India; there is no single specific Dzogchen term which can have been translated from Sanskrit or another Indian language.[29] In the Nyingma tradition they surely mention Guru Rinpoche but there is a lot of discussion as to where he

---

[26] Tib. Srong btsan Sgam po / སྲོང་བཙན་སྒམ་པོ།

[27] Tib. Rnying ma, Bka' rgyud, Sa skya, Dge lugs / རྙིང་མ། བཀའ་བརྒྱུད། ས་སྐྱ། དགེ་ལུགས།

[28] Tib. theg pa rim dgu / ཐེག་པ་རིམ་དགུ

[29] Samten Chhosphel, *Exposition of the Nine Vehicles (According to the Nyingma and Bon Traditions)*, Miscellaneous Series – 21, Bsam gtan chos phel, *Gsang sngags rnying ma dang g.yung drung bon gyi lugs gnyis las byung ba'i theg rim pa dgu'i rnam bzhag*, (Sarnath,Varanasi: Central Institute of Higher Tibetan Studies: 2006), pp. 603-604.

really came from. It is hard to say; there is a lot of discussion about this, but it is not clear at all and I would rather not go into this subject.

Similarly, within the Buddhist tradition, the Abhidharma cosmology[30] which is said to have come from the North or West, from regions which are nowadays Kashmir, Pakistan or Afghanistan, was taught by authors such as Asanga and Vasubandhu.[31] Now there is the question of whether these things were originally included in the words of Buddha Shakyamuni or not. This should be checked. Nowadays researching and discussing such matters is permitted, especially in the Sarnath Institute in Varanasi, where students are trained for the *acharya* degree. There are five Bönpo *geshes* and thirty-three Bönpo students studying there, and now, on the insistence of H.H. the Dalai Lama, ideas can be exchanged freely. There is open discussion on such matters.

As regards the source of the teachings, Buddhist teachings are supposed to have originated from India while Bön teachings are said to have originated from Zhang Zhung. So we can say that there were two main religions in Tibet: Bön and Buddhism. Areas such as

---

[30] Tib. mdzod phug / མཛོད་ཕུག །

[31] The half-brothers Asanga and Vasubandhu are very important Buddhist scholars considered to be the cofounders of the Mahayana School of Yogachara. Asanga was born in Purushapura, present day Peshawar in Pakistan. Vasubandhu was born in Gandhara, modern day Allahabad in Uttar Pradesh, Northern India. He then studied in Kashmir. Both masters studied and practised in the wider north-western Himalayan region which is also associated with the kingdoms of Zhang Zhung and Uddiyana. According to Yungdrung Bön scriptures, many Yungdrung Bön teachings have been spread in this region since very archaic times and are known under the general name *Gyagar Bönkor* [Tib. gya gar bon skor / རྒྱ་གར་བོན་སྐོར །], *The Indian Bön Cycle*. According to Yongdzin Rinpoche, in this case 'Indian' refers to the Himalaya. There is ongoing debate as to whether Mahayana was taught by Shakyamuni Buddha. Some Western scholars such as Prof. R. Gombrich maintain that Hinayana alone is the authentic teaching of Shakyamuni Buddha. This then begs the question: What are the origins of Mahayana? Since many Mahayana and Vajrayana teachings are associated with the north-western Himalayan region and Central Asia, and since this is precisely where Yungdrung Bön was spread, Mahayana and Vajrayana may well represent a blend of Indian Buddhism and Yungdrung Bön doctrines.

Kinnaur, Spiti and Ladakh to the West of Mount Kailash all previously formed part of the Zhang Zhung kingdom. Now it is quite clear that there was a Zhang Zhung language, and such subjects can be freely researched. A dictionary of Zhang Zhung terms has been compiled,[32] and it is becoming quite clear that these teachings of Yungdrung Bön cannot have come from India but in fact did indeed come originally from Zhang Zhung. The system of the Nine Vehicles clearly comes from Zhang Zhung, and the highest of the nine is called the Unsurpassable Summit, Lame Thegpa,[33] which is actually Dzogchen. Previously, there were many who said that the Bönpos had no authentic source for their teachings, but now this is a thing of the past; there is no question of that any more.

There is much to say about this, but we will not elaborate any longer. Suffice to say, this and similar centres have now been established in Europe.

Preliminary Practices as a foundation for Dzogchen

It is very important to establish this centre here, which is mainly a centre for the teaching of Dzogchen by Khenpo Rinpoche, who is very good, and you should study well. In order to practise Dzogchen, we

---

[32] To date, several dictionaries of Zhang Zhung terms have been compiled with various language combinations: Siegbert Hummel, Tr. Guido Vogliotti, *On Zhang-zhung*, (LTWA, Dharamasala, 2000); Dagkar Namgyal Nyima, *Zhang-zhung – Tibetan – English Contextual Dictionary*, (Self-published, Bonn, 2003) ISBN: 3-00-012012-2; Comp. Pasar Tsultrim Tenzin, Changru Tritsuk Namdak Nyima, Gatsa Lodroe Rabsal, Ed. Yasuhiko Nagano, Samten G. Karmay, Tr. Heather Stoddard, *A Lexicon of Zhang Zhung and Bonpo Terms*, (Senri Ethnological Reports 76, Bon Studies 11, National Museum of Ethnology, Osaka, 2008); Ed. Tsuguhito Takeuchi, Burkhard Quessel, Yasuhiko Nagano, *Research Notes on the Zhangzhung Language by Frederick W. Thomas at the British Library*, Senri Ethnological Reports 99, Bon Studies 14, National Museum of Ethnology, Osaka, 2011).

[33] Tib. Bla med theg pa / བླ་མེད་ཐེག་པ།

all know that the basis or the ground we must establish is that of the Preliminary Practices.

Yongdzin Rinpoche is a very great Dzogchen Master. He is the most authentic and qualified Master, a very special Master. There is no-one at all in the Bön tradition who can be compared to him. The monasteries of Menri and Triten Norbutse were founded in early times, and it is very important to keep *vinaya* there. Since then, many other centres have been established, and now Shenten Dargye Ling has also been inaugurated. It is very important to focus on Dzogchen here. Now there are many disciples, and my request to you is that you study and practise the Preliminary Practices very thoroughly; even though Dzogchen is very important, the Preliminary Practices are very important, too. The purpose of practising Dzogchen is to dissolve ego-grasping and, as we are bound with self-grasping thought, we have to be very careful about this. If one is strongly bound with this grasping, it is not possible to realize the Natural State of Dzogchen, therefore, from the beginning, one has to train and practise the Preliminary Practices very carefully, as you are doing here, during the 100 day *gomdra* [34] retreat last year, for example. It is not easy for this to be done in other places, but you have managed it here and that is excellent.

The highest teachings require qualified students, so we must become qualified students through the practice of the Preliminaries, through proper study and so on. I very much rejoice in the *gomdra* retreat cycle which has started in Shenten now. Moreover, this place is very well-suited to the practice of Dzogchen – it is very open and pleasant. In Tibet it was not always easy and the Bönpos had to hide on high mountain peaks or in little corners; they had to hide, you see,

---

[34] Tib. sgom grwa / སྒོམ་གྲྭ། – Meditation School.

because there were many problems and persecutions. It was not as comfortable as it is here!

Nowadays there is also a growing number of Chinese people who are becoming interested in Bön. This is true for the field of medicine, too. In the Bön tradition we have the *Bumzhi*, while the Buddhists have the *Gyudzhi*, the Four Tantras.[35] The *Bumzhi* used to be completely unknown or despised, but now it is regarded with great interest and is an object of research everywhere, including Tibet and China.

Nowadays many lamas from Tibet are making contact with India, China, Europe and America, looking for ways to connect and collaborate. Everyone hopes and requests that this centre, Shenten Dargye Ling, will be a stable, well-developed seat where Bön can flourish so that this place can become a great resource for Bönpos everywhere. I don't call all centres monasteries as a monastery has to be based on monastic rule and the rules of *vinaya* must be kept. A centre or institute, on the other hand, is open to all. When the Bönpo lamas gathered in India, they founded the Menri monastery, and now the *ngagpa* or lay practitioners' *gompa* is also being established alongside this, as well as a separate convent which has been set up for nuns. The base of the teachings is the same. The Ngagpa Gompa welcomes everyone, but as for the monastery, that follows the *vinaya* rules. The nuns also follow the *vinaya* rules. The *yogis* and *yoginis* are free; they don't need to go through the *vinaya* rule. They go directly to the Dzogchen rule!

---

[35] The Bumzhi [Tib. 'Bum gzhi / འབུམ་གཞི།] are the Four Medical Tantras of the Yungdrung Bön tradition which are now widely accepted as being the original source of the better-known Gyudzhi [Tib. Rgyud bzhi / རྒྱུད་བཞི།], the Four Medical Tantras of the Tibetan Buddhist tradition.

But anyway, it is very important to first practise the Preliminaries properly. In order to feel disenchanted with *samsara*,[36] one should think deeply on impermanence. Meditation on impermanence is extremely important because it is thanks to this that the knot of ego-grasping, *ngadzin*,[37] can be released. From this, one can proceed to the next step, Refuge and Bodhichitta, which are the gateway through which one enters the path. In order to gather the accumulations of merits and wisdom, one should make the Mandala Offering. In order to receive the blessings in the right way one should pray in the right way. These Preliminary Practices are that which ripens the unripe mind. One should understand the suffering of others and oneself; by recognizing one's own suffering, one develops a feeling of renunciation towards *samsara*. By recognizing the suffering of others, one develops a feeling of compassion. Then, following on from this, one develops a confident faith in the Three Jewels, and, on this basis, one takes Refuge. In order to develop renunciation and establish it firmly, one must realize the sufferings of *samsara* and all the various types of suffering of the lower realms. The real Dzogchen practice, remaining in the state of equanimity without any duality of you and me, this is great. But don't be in a rush to enter this path. One must rest firmly upon the base of the Preliminary Practices and tame one's own mind. That is very important. It is very important to dissolve self-grasping. We should turn our minds towards practice, and, in order to do so, we must clearly distinguish what is virtuous and what is non-virtuous. We should recognize ego-grasping for what it is, and get rid of it.

We are talking about meditation; meditation is *gom*[38] in Tibetan, and that means 'to become familiar with.' When we become familiar with practice, then, at any of the four times – while we are

---

[36] Tib. 'khor ba / འཁོར་བ།

[37] Tib. nga 'dzin / ང་འཛིན།

[38] Tib. sgom / སྒོམ།

walking, eating, sleeping, or sitting – we will naturally become stable with the practice. One must be constantly aware, and develop awareness. If one becomes more mindful and aware, then one will naturally develop *rigpai rangtsug*[39] which is the Natural State of Self-Awareness, *rigpa*.[40]

There is a lot to say, but my main wish is that, since you already have received this tradition of the Preliminary Practices, you would practise them in the proper way and become familiar with them, and with Guru Yoga in particular. If you become familiar with the two last verses of the Guru Yoga prayer, that is sufficient:

།སངས་རྒྱས་སེམས་སུ་སྟོན་པ་རིན་པོ་ཆེ།

SANG-GYE SEM SU TÖN-PA RIN-PO-CHE
Precious Jewel who introduces Buddha Nature,

།རང་ངོ་རང་གི་ཤེས་པར་བྱིན་གྱི་རློབས།

RANG-NGO-RANG GI SHE-PAR JYIN GYI LOB
Bless me so that I may realize my own Self-Aware State![41]

You already know these lines, and if you focus on them, then the realization of the Natural State of the Mind will naturally manifest.

Refuge

Our practice rests upon Refuge and Bodhichitta, which are in turn based upon renunciation. Why is this? As for Refuge, it can be defined as 'seeking protection.' Protection from what? Protection from *samsara*. So actually, *ngejung*,[42] renunciation, is some sort of fear

---

[39] Tib. rig pa'i rang tshugs / རིག་པའི་རང་ཚུགས།

[40] Tib. rig pa / རིག་པ།

[41] Translation by Nagru Geshe Gelek Jinpa and Dmitry Ermakov. First published in *Tummo: A Practice Manual by Shardza Tashi Gyaltsen*, Shenten Dargye Ling, France, 2006.

[42] Tib. nges 'byung / ངེས་འབྱུང་།

which comes from realizing what the sufferings of *samsara* are, either for oneself or for others. One seeks protection for oneself and therefore takes Refuge, and then compassion arises from the wish to protect others from the sufferings of *samsara*. This renunciation is the root or the cause of the motivation which leads one to take refuge. Based on this, we should have firm faith in the objects of Refuge.

The objects of Refuge

As for the objects of Refuge, you know them already. We say: 'I take Refuge in the Masters. I take Refuge in the Buddhas. I take Refuge in Yungdrung Bön. I take Refuge in the Shenrab Yungdrung Sempa,[43] in the Sangha.' Or, we take Refuge in the Three Roots[44] as we recited this morning: 'I take Refuge in the Lama, the Yidam[45] and the Khandro.'[46] This is more in keeping with the style of Tantra. But either way, we should in fact visualize the Refuge Tree as you have all seen it on *thangkas*. We visualize this in the sky in front of us with a great sense of respect and inspiration.

I think it would be proper to introduce you to all the characters of the Refuge Tree in more detail.

In the sky in front of us, in a vast and auspicious array of wonders, on the top of a throne supported by eight lions, on cushions of a lotus, sun and moon we should visualize the one whose nature gathers the essence of all the Buddhas of the Three Times and the Ten Directions, He is bight and shining as a snowy mountain.

---

[43] Tib. Gshen rab g.yung drung sems dpa' / གཤེན་རབ་གཡུང་དྲུང་སེམས་དཔའ།

[44] Tib. rtsa gsum / རྩ་གསུམ།

[45] Tib. yi dam / ཡི་དམ།

[46] Tib. bla ma yi dam mkha' 'gro / བླ་མ། ཡི་དམ། མཁའ་འགྲོ།

Fig. 2 Refuge Tree of Yungdrung Bön. Photo courtesy Christophe Moulin.

Fig. 3 Shenlha Wökar. Photo courtesy Christophe Moulin.

We must visualize Shenlha Wökar[47] with one face and two arms, with his legs crossed and his hands in the mudra of meditation. He has the nine manners of purity and is adorned with the thirteen peaceful ornaments of a *sambhogakaya*[48] form. We should visualize this clearly in front of us.

The nine manners of purity:
His body is:
1. youthful;
2. bright and;
3. luminous;
4. with a clear lustre.
His manner is:
5. peaceful;
6. his limbs are supple and
7. flexible.
He is:
8. beautiful and
9. blazing with splendour.

The thirteen adornments of a peaceful *sambhogakaya*:[49]
1. Crown;
2. Earrings;
3. Short necklace;
4. Medium necklace;
5. Long necklace;
6. Bracelets;
7. Bracelets on the upper part of the arm;
8. Anklets;
9. Shawl;
10. Lower garment;
11. An umbrella above;

---

[47] Tib. Gshen lha 'od dkar / གཤེན་ལྷ་འོད་དཀར།
[48] Tib. long sku / ལོང་སྐུ།
[49] Tib. longs sku'i rgyan chas bcu gsum / ལོངས་སྐུའི་རྒྱན་ཆས་བཅུ་གསུམ།

12. A back- and headrest behind the throne;
13. The throne.

We should know these perfectly as they are common to all peaceful *sambhogakaya* forms as well as to those in this Refuge Tree.

Shenlha Wökar represents the Root Lama.[50] On his right we should imagine all the *mandalas* of the peaceful and wrathful deities. Above this are the Thousand and One Buddhas of the good *kalpa*.[51] To his left are the Masing Khandro,[52] the *dakini*. Above these are the Yungdrung Sempas[53] or *bodhisattvas* of Mahayana, the Great Vehicle, those who abide in the Five Paths[54] and the Ten Bhumis.[55] Behind Shenlha Wökar are the supports of the Three Jewels which represent the objects of Refuge: statues, scriptures and stupas. Above his head are all the lamas of the lineage of the Great Vehicle. In the centre are the lamas of the *Zhang Zhung Nyengyud*.[56] To the left of this are the lamas of *Dzogchen Dragpa Korsum*.[57] In the first line to the right are the *Athri*[58] lamas. All these are Dzogchen Lineage Masters who obtained Rainbow Body.[59] The second line to the left depicts the lamas of the Secret Mantra[60] or Tantras, and the second

---

[50] Tib. rtsa ba'i bla ma / རྩ་བའི་བླ་མ། – a most important master, the one who introduces the practitioner to the Nature of Mind, as well as imparting various transmissions, explanations, empowerments and blessings pertaining to the lineage one is following. A student should check a potential master thoroughly, just as a master should check a potential student. Traditionally, this process should take seven-twelve years.

[51] Tib. bskal pa / བསྐལ་པ།

[52] Tib. ma sring mkha' 'gro / མ་སྲིང་མཁའ་འགྲོ། – Mother and Sister *dakini*.

[53] Tib. g.yung drung sems dpa' / གཡུང་དྲུང་སེམས་དཔའ།

[54] Tib. lam lnga / ལམ་ལྔ།

[55] Tib. sa bcu / ས་བཅུ།

[56] Tib. Zhang zhung snyan rgyud / ཞང་ཞུང་སྙན་རྒྱུད།

[57] Tib. Rdzogs chen grags pa skor gsum / རྫོགས་ཆེན་གྲགས་པ་སྐོར་གསུམ།

[58] Tib. A khrid / ཨ་ཁྲིད།

[59] Tib. 'ja' lus / འཇའ་ལུས།

[60] Tib. gsang sngags / གསང་སྔགས།

line to the right depicts the lamas of the *vinaya*[61] lineage. The lineages all come up to Kuntu Zangpo.[62]

In front of [below] our Root Lama is a row of Protectors with Sidpai Gyalmo[63] in the centre flanked by the male protectors on her right and the female protectors on her left. The function of the Protectors is to dispel all obstacles or unfavourable circumstances which may arise for the practitioner.

Then, having visualized all this, we respectfully offer the *mandala*, and prostrate with the five parts of our body. When we touch our knees, hands and head to the ground we consider we are thus purified of what is to be rejected, i.e. the Two Obscurations.[64] When we stand up again, we think we are receiving all the qualities of what is to be realized. This is a kind of doorway or the foundation of all practice, and we should have a confident, stable and inspired faith in the objects of Refuge.

Actually, we should know all these details very precisely. When we take Refuge, we should visualize our father and all male beings on our right and our mother along with all female beings on our left. Thus we think that we are all taking Refuge together. We do not have time to go into all the details now, but they are in the texts and we should know all this properly and clearly from reading the text or teachings we have received. We should gradually train ourselves in visualizing this clearly as it is in fact this foundation which we use when we take Refuge, when we generate Bodhichitta and also when

---

[61] Tib. 'dul ba / འདུལ་བ།

[62] Tib. Kun tu bzang po / ཀུན་ཏུ་བཟང་པོ།

[63] Tib. Srid pa'i rgyal mo / སྲིད་པའི་རྒྱལ་མོ།

[64] Tib. sgrib pa gnyis / སྒྲིབ་པ་གཉིས། – the obscuration of emotions and [intellectual] knowledge.

we make Mandala Offering. All these practices, as well as Guru Yoga, are based on this same visualization.

It would be very good if each of you could keep a good picture of the Refuge Tree close by you, always, so that you can train in visualizing this. It is good to keep a copy of the Refuge Tree by your bed, for instance.

We should really know this very precisely, with all the details of the Refuge Tree. Everything is described properly in the text, even down to the appearance of each individual lama. They are described in the proper order, the deities are all described precisely and even each Protector in the rows of Protectors is described precisely, in the right place. We should be able to visualize all these in their own place. This is extremely important, especially for those following the *gomdra* programme; you should be competent and able to visualize all these things because this is the basis of your practice. This is not only the basis of Guru Yoga but also of Confession and so on.

The Refuge Tree should not only be visualized during the sessions, but also in between sessions. For example, when we are engaged in any of the four activities of sitting, walking, lying or eating – or sleeping or working – we must visualize them, too. When we are seated we should visualize them in front of us. When we are eating we must consider we are making offerings to them. When we are walking we should visualize them above our left shoulder – in this way we are making *kora*,[65] in the Bönpo way. We can say this is the natural way. The earth is turning this way, the moon is turning this way – all the other planets go this way. Only sun goes the other way.[66]

---

[65] Tib. skor ra / སྐོར་ར། – circumambulation.

[66] As we see it from the Earth, the Sun goes clockwise in its daily path but its yearly movement along the ecliptic is actually counter clockwise, as seen from the Northern Hemisphere.

In early times, one professor in Europe said: 'anti,' anti-clockwise. But I say it is natural![67]

Vows

When we take Refuge, there are vows. There are also Bodhisattva vows. It is very important to take and observe these, and we can ask our Khenpo Rinpoche to explain and give us these vows. Some people think this is not important, but in fact it would be a very good base for Dzogchen, since we should not just jump into Dzogchen without any preparation. It is better to enter into Dzogchen gradually and properly, and then our practice will develop in a good way. It is all well and good to be inspired by the practice of Dzogchen, but, actually, Dzogchen is a very high practice and we should not think of going straight there; we must realize that it is very high and we must prepare ourselves for it gradually.

For example, Dzogchen is the final subject even for monks who are studying for the *geshe* degree; they don't go straight into it. One shouldn't hurry or rush into Dzogchen thinking: 'Oh, I must learn quickly and then I want to teach others and then gather many disciples and become famous!' One should ground oneself and make a stable foundation. If one has a good foundation then the realization of Dzogchen will be quicker, faster and more stable.

I shouldn't say Dzogchen is very high. I should say it is 'easy.' Dzogchen is very easy. But to arrive there safely, you should go safely, slowly, slowly, not in a hurry. If you rush you cannot reach it; if you go slowly, you will reach it quickly. If you go very fast, you cannot reach it!

Do you have any questions?

---

[67] In Tibetan it is simply called Tib. g.yas skor / གཡས་སྐོར། – turning to the right.

Q: Could His Holiness grant us the Refuge and Bodhichitta vows?

A: There is no special need – maybe you have already received them from Yongdzin Rinpoche or Khenpo Rinpoche and anyway, if you receive the empowerment of Jamma[68] which will be given in a few days, they are included so you will get them. When we talk about vows, there is also commitment, so once you have received a vow, you should not forget it, you must observe it. So, for example, we should take Refuge six times a day, or three times a day, or at the very least, twice a day, when we wake up and when we go to bed. One should recite the Refuge prayer regularly. When we use the term 'vow' it means something we have to keep strictly. So if, for example, one takes ordination as a monk one should respect the four root vows and the two hundred and some branch vows. These really should be kept; one should not waver or get distracted or forget them, one should keep them. So, in the same way, when we speak of *dompa*, 'vow' or *damtsig*,[69] 'commitment,' these should be kept.

For example, once one has taken Refuge in the Lama one should not seek refuge in any worldly beings with the hope of attaining Buddhahood. Once one has taken Refuge in the Buddha one should not seek refuge in worldly gods. Once one has taken Refuge in Bön one should not harm any other being or denigrate any other religious schools. Once one has taken Refuge in the Bodhisattvas or the Yungdrung Sempas one should not follow mistaken views. This is the twenty-first century, so everyone has to make friends with everyone else! It is a little bit difficult. Vows are a little bit difficult. In the early times vows were very important. Now, everyone is friends, we are all equal, all one class. It is good; being friends with

---

[68] Tib. 'Byams ma / འབྱམས་མ།

[69] Tib. sdom pa, dam tshig / སྡོམ་པ། དམ་ཚིག

everyone, it looks as though we are developing the enlightened mind of Mahayana!

To conclude for today, my main advice is to practise the Preliminary Practices seriously and to be focussed on their meaning with great devotion and respect. If you practise in this way, the Preliminaries will be very beneficial. If we just recite a lot but our mind is elsewhere or we do not have the intention to rid ourselves of ego-grasping, then the Preliminary Practices might be of some benefit but not so much; it will take a long time to obtain the result of practice. But if you recite a prayer ten times with great devotion then it is much better than reciting it 100 times with distraction. So when we practise we must do so with devotion, and, as a result, in this life you will have the benefit of a long life without obstacles or sickness, and your virtuous activities will be successful.

Bodhichitta

We have finished the explanation of Refuge. Now let us move to the next subject. In order to gain the precious state of the fully enlightened Buddha, we must first generate the Mind of Enlightenment, *bodhichitta*. This is the entrance to Mahayana. Therefore, let us now generate the mind of *bodhichitta*.

When we generate the thought of *bodhichitta* we should think of all these objects of Refuge and pray: 'Please, all of you, behold us, hear us and be our witness as we generate *bodhichitta*.'

We should think that all the *swastika* objects of Refuge are in front of us, i.e. the lamas, the Buddhas, the teachings of Yungdrung Bön, the Yungdrung Sempas, *yidams* and *khandros*. These are all gathered in front of us, blazing with splendour, exceedingly luminous and beautiful. We should imagine that they are actually in front of us in the sky. We should not only think vaguely that they are here; we should visualize them very clearly. Why? Because they are the witnesses of our *bodhichitta* commitment. When we speak of Refuge, it is sort of for our own benefit – we are taking Refuge in order to be protected from the ills of sa*m*sara. But when we come to Bodhichitta, the Refuge Tree is the witness of the commitment we are taking for the sake of all sentient beings.

All sentient beings are our mother

We should think that among all those infinite beings who are wandering in *samsara*, there is not one which has not been our loving father or mother. We should consider the fact that, as we have been taking rebirth in *samsara* since beginningless time, all sentient beings must have been our mother at some point. Thus we should consider that, just as we are grateful to our parents of this life for their kindness, so, too, we should be grateful to all our parents of all our infinite past lives for their kindness.

Parents are held in high esteem, at least according to our old tradition. This is because they have fed us and taken care of us since our childhood. They have given us clothes and everything we need. Thus it is impossible to repay their kindness. If we were to carry them upon our head, circle the whole world thrice and then carry them up to the Land of Pure Bliss, even this would be insufficient to repay their kindness. In the West, people may have a strong reaction to this, but in fact, we cannot repay our parents' kindness.

Repaying our mothers' kindness

So if even carrying them thrice around the world and bringing them up to the Land of Pure Bliss, Dewachen[70] is not enough, how can we repay their kindness? The only way is to train in the Bodhichitta of the Great Vehicle, by training in this visualization and by generating the intention to bring them and all sentient beings to ultimate

---

[70] Tib. Bde ba can / བདེ་བ་ཅན།

liberation. This is called 'developing the mind of Enlightenment of Mahayana,' the Great Vehicle.

We should think: 'As for those sentient beings who are wandering lost and blind in the darkness of *samsara* with no guide to lead them to ultimate peace, as for all these loving mothers of our past lives, they are deprived of a guide to lead them to ultimate happiness, they desperately need a guide, a Master, someone who can lead them. As they have no guide, I, myself, shall now promise to lead all my mothers to ultimate peace and happiness. But how can I do so? They need ultimate liberation – may they obtain it before me! May they obtain full and perfect enlightenment even before I do! It would not be proper if I only obtained liberation for myself.'

Thinking in this way, we really generate *bodhichitta*, the mind of Enlightenment.

In fact, there have already been a great many Buddhas and *bodhisattvas*, but all of them gained this high realization and were able to accomplish such immense activities for the sake of all sentient beings by resting on this firm foundation of *bodhichitta*: 'May all sentient beings gain enlightenment even before I do.'

We should also wish to obtain enlightenment in this very lifetime; it is not a question of obtaining it sometime in the future. We should think: 'May I find a way to establish each and every sentient being, without a single exception, in the state of full and perfect enlightenment, without overlooking even a single one.' We should not merely think this once or twice; we should train in this intention. We should make prayers and aspirations with our mind fully focussed on this. While generating this thought, we should consider that all the Buddhas and deities of the Refuge Tree are actually present in front of us as our witness. They are not merely a painting but are alive and clear, with non-material, luminous bodies.

Let us do this now, all together. Let us visualize the Refuge Tree clearly in front of us and recite the Bodhichitta prayer:

གསང་བ་གསང་ཆེན་གསང་མཆོག་མཐར་ཐུག་རྒྱལ།

SANG-WA SANG-CHEN SANG-CHOG THAR-THUG GYAL

The King of the Final Goal is the mysterious, exceedingly secret, sublime essence,

གསང་མཆོག་ཡིད་བཞིན་ཐུགས་ཀྱི་ནོར་བུ་ལ།

SANG-CHOG YI-ZHIN THUG KYI NOR-BU LA

Into this great secret yidam *whose mind is the precious wish full-filling jewel of the Nature of Mind,*

བདག་ཉིད་ལེགས་འཇུག་འགྲོ་ཀུན་འདྲེན་པར་བགྱི།

DAG-NYI LEG JUG DRO-KÜN DREN-PAR GYI'I

I enter [happily] to guide all sentient beings [to Buddhahood];

མཐའ་ཡས་སེམས་ཅན་དོན་ཕྱིར་སེམས་བསྐྱེད་དོ།

THA-YE SEM-CHEN-DÖN CHYIR SEM-KYED DO

I generate bodhichitta *to benefit infinite sentient beings.*[71]

When we recite this prayer, we should do so with the resolute intention: 'May I obtain Buddhahood in this very lifetime for the sake of all sentient beings.' *Bodhichitta* is actually something which should be meditated upon, and one way to do this is to accumulate one hundred recitations of the prayer we have just been chanting. Here we have a very pleasant, comfortable, quiet place which is well suited to practice, and when we are all gathered here together it is of great benefit if we recite these words together. Traditionally, we must recite these prayers of Refuge, Bodhichitta and so on one hundred thousand

---

[71] Translation by Yongdzin Lopön Tenzin Namdak Rinpoche and Dmitry Ermakov. First published in *The Secret Practice of Khöpung Drenpa's Innermost Essence*, FPYB, UK, 2013.

times when we do *ngöndro*[72] practice. But when we unite and chant these prayers together, it has more power and we can receive more blessings. Therefore, it is very important to recite these prayers from time to time in the assembly of all the practitioners.

Moreover, in a large gathering there may be all sorts of people including *bodhisattvas* or *trülkus*[73] or *nirmanakayas*. There are many unrecognized 'Supreme Nirmanakayas,'[74] emanations for the sake of all sentient beings. When we recite prayers together, all the merit is gathered and pooled; each person shares the merit, so the advantage is very great.

When we see a large gathering of people we might think that they have assembled here without reason. When so many people gather from different continents and countries, we have never ever met before, yet we naturally feel close and smile at each other and have some kind of happy feeling. We older people always think that this comes from past karma and past prayers and aspirations, especially when people gather to recite prayers or receive teachings. Young people think it is a question of advertising and publicity which attracts people, but we think differently. In modern times we try to introduce ourselves to each other, exchanging business cards or something. But actually, this is not necessary; especially in this kind of gathering: we are meeting together due to our previous meritorious karma and virtues. We have to give this more weight. I believe this!

Dissolving the visualization

After having generated the visualization of the Refuge Tree very clearly, at the end of the session we must dissolve it. All the sentient beings are gathered or dissolved into oneself, while the deities

---

[72] Tib. sngon 'gro / སྔོན་འགྲོ།
[73] Tib. sprul sku / སྤྲུལ་སྐུ།
[74] Tib. mchog sprul / མཆོག་སྤྲུལ།

gradually dissolve into each other one by one and then finally into Shenlha Wökar like the steam of one's breath vanishing from a mirror. The lamas and deities slowly melt or fuse into the central figure of Shenlha Wökar, and then, finally, Shenlha Wökar dissolves into oneself. At this moment, we must think with gratitude that we have now development ultimate *bodhichitta*. We remain in a state free from all grasping and dualistic thoughts.

Dedication

Then we should think that, just as all the Buddhas and *bodhisattvas* have done, so we, too, dedicate all the virtues we have accumulated through this practice that each and every sentient being may attain full and perfect Buddhahood. We should then recite many prayers and aspiration prayers for the sake of all sentient beings, but in particular we should pray that we may realize the perfect View of Dzogchen, which is unsurpassable. This is the essential point for which we are now preparing. All these practices such as Refuge, Bodhichitta, Mandala Offering, Confession and so on are preparations for realizing this perfect View of Dzogchen.

The Preliminaries Practice: an important base

It is a pity we cannot go into all the details of the Refuge Tree, but you will have other opportunities for this. Anyway, you should do the visualization very clearly, then take Refuge and, as I have explained, develop *bodhichitta*. It is also in front of this same Refuge Tree that we make confession, offer the *mandala* and practise Guru Yoga. We should definitely accumulate all the nine hundred thousand of recitations, that is, one hundred thousand for each of the nine stages of the Preliminaries. This is a very solid and safe foundation for realizing Dzogpa Chenpo.[75] If we prepare this strong and stable foundation then it is said that the View of Dzogchen will unfold

---

[75] Tib Rdzogs pa chen po / རྫོགས་པ་ཆེན་པོ།

naturally. It is impossible for it not to unfold in us, since, irrespective of our qualities, each and every one of us is endowed with this Nature; it will surely manifest if we prepare properly.

We all have some duties and have to go to work, but no matter what our work is, even if we are extremely busy, we should maintain this practice. Even if we are extremely busy, we can always find a few minutes – if not five then at least two or three – every morning and evening to do this visualization, take Refuge, develop *bodhichitta* and so on. We should keep up with this practice as much as we can, at all times. Even if we are at work, we can remember and do this practice inwardly. This is the least we can do, and it is impossible not to be able to do this.

Refuge as protection

Taking Refuge is very important. It is that which protects us, and we should think of it as our protection. Even if some obstacles arise in our life or work, we should focus on our Refuge and think that this will protect us from obstacles. In our ordinary daily life, work and so on, all sorts of unfavourable circumstances may arise, but on no account should we think: 'Oh, I have nobody to protect me. Nobody will help me. I am alone.' No, you are not alone. You are protected and it is the objects of Refuge who afford you this protection. Taking Refuge will protect you from any type of obstacles which may occur. You should not forget the objects of Refuge even when you throw a party. You should also be able to remember your Refuge if you have some great fears. No matter what conditions you are facing, you should always remind yourself of Refuge practice and not break this.

So we have explained taking Refuge and how to develop *bodhichitta*. This teaching must be listened to very carefully. Not only should we listen to it very carefully, we should also try to trust it. We should not only trust it but we should also have faith in it, real faith, and really believe that the Three Jewels never fail us. But it depends on our trust. If we have strong trust and if, on our side, we do our best to practise Refuge, then they will never fail us.

Controlling the mind, the most important of the Three Gates

We are made up of three aspects: body, speech and mind. We can do things with our body and with our speech, and we can use our mind to think. However, the main, essential point is what we do with our mind. We can perform positive or negative actions with our body, speech or mind, but ultimately it all traces back to the mind, to its will to instigate something good, to encourage others to do good or to rejoice in the good deeds of others. Finally, all this goes back to the intention of the mind. We can perform either negative or positive activities with our body, speech and mind, but out of these three, body and speech are like servants while the mind is the most powerful component; it makes the other two act. Therefore, the mind is most important, and so we must take care of our mind.

Whether we perform virtuous or negative acts, finally the responsibility lies with our mind. Whether we perform positive actions ourselves, whether we ask others to do them or whether we rejoice in the good deeds of others, the benefit for us is the same.

The actions of the body and speech are easier to control, but who is there to control the actions of the mind? Who can control the mind? It is quite easy to control the body; we can assume a certain posture if we decide to. We can also control our speech; it is easy to stop speaking if we decide to do so. But it is much more difficult to control the mind. If it is possible to control our mind then there should be a controller, someone who controls it. So then, who is the one who controls our mind? In order to control it, we must recognize its nature; that is the way to control it. All the so-called Preliminary Practices are the mind's duty; they mostly depend on the mind – it is the mind which should take Refuge and develop *bodhichitta*. The only way to control the mind is through what we have been teaching about Refuge, *bodhichitta* and many other practices which you have been doing and will do in the future. This is the way to control our mind. Not only our mind but also our body and speech. It is especially beneficial if we remember this first thing in the morning when we wake up and last thing at night when we go to bed. In this way, our sleep will be very quiet and all our activities will be full of positive motivation, positive aspirations.

These days we read so many books. You can read many books about spiritual practices as well as many books about general topics such as science and mathematics. By reading books you can gain certain understanding and many different concepts, but there is no end to this. The more you read, the more understanding you gain, but still you can always find something else which is interesting, something else which you have not yet understood. If you keep going in this way, there is no end. So therefore it is good to concentrate more on meditation and contemplation. If you do this, it will open a certain way to recognize your own Natural State of the Mind. If on the other hand you just rely on reading books, there is no end.

Combining the practice of Dzogchen with Refuge and Bodhichitta

The main thing is meditation, and out of all the different types of meditation, the main one is the meditation of Dzogchen. When you know one thing, everything will liberate. That is the Natural State of the Mind. Here, we are in an extremely favourable situation. We have an outstanding Master, the place is excellent, very quiet and comfortable. If we were to combine the practice of Dzogchen with the practice of taking Refuge and developing *bodhichitta*, then the blessing would be tremendous and the power of the practice would be very great. So let us make the most of the very good circumstances we have here. This is my wish. This is what we need – we need to be liberated!

Integrating practice with work

We all have to go to work, but we should consider that if we go to work and do our job honestly and well, then this is not opposed to the practice of virtue; this is also good action, a good practice. We definitely have to go to work. There is work and practice, but they are complimentary, just as we have the left and right hands, the left and right legs, and we need them both to walk. Or we have the left eye and the right eye and we need them both to see. Here we are not talking about negative actions; we are talking about positive actions, and our work is necessary. We can combine our work with developing *bodhichitta* and that is a very good way.

Questions and Answers

Q: My personal background is in the Kagyud and Nyingma lineages of Tibetan Buddhism and I don't know Bön at all. So I would like to know if, in your experience, Mahamudra also exists in the Bön tradition. Mahamudra means that everything has the seal of bliss and emptiness.[76] Do you have this in Bön?

A: Yes, for example in the Kagyud system there is this so-called Mahamudra, Chyaggya Chenpo.[77] In the Gelug system there is the so-called Uma Chenpo,[78] Great Madhyamaka. In the Sakya tradition there is the great Lamdre,[79] the Path with its Fruit, and in the Nyingma and Bön traditions we have Dzogpa Chenpo, the Great Perfection. As I explained yesterday, in the University of Varanasi in Sarnath, they have gathered scholars from the four branches of Buddhism with the Bönpos as the fifth, and together they have been researching Dzogpa Chenpo. After thorough research, it appears that there is no single

---

[76] Tib. bde stong / བདེ་སྟོང་།

[77] Tib. phyag rgya chen po / ཕྱག་རྒྱ་ཆེན་པོ།

[78] Tib. dbu ma chen po / དབུ་མ་ཆེན་པོ།

[79] Tib. lam 'bras / ལམ་འབྲས།

word of Dzogchen in the Gelug tradition. There is no single word of Dzogchen in the Sakya tradition, nor in the Kagyud. As for the Nyingma tradition, the teachings are said to come from Guru Rinpoche, but who knows. These Tibetan scholars also collaborated with Indian Pandita scholars and through their joint research and discussions they discovered that there is no single word of Dzogchen in any Indian sources at all. So this is a genuine Tibetan tradition. That was their conclusion.[80]

His Holiness the XIV Dalai Lama says that in Tibet there were two religions: that of the Bönpo and that of the Bande,[81] the Buddhists. We should be able to trace everything that is Buddhist to India and everything Bön to Zhang Zhung. A lot of research has been done by many important scholars as to the history and origins of these things and this work is continuing. Tibetologists used to think that there was nothing in Tibet prior to the arrival of Buddhism, that there was just complete darkness, and that everything grew and developed from the introduction of Buddhism. They thought it was a cultural desert prior to this. In fact, this is not the case. Even H.H. the Dalai Lama says that Bön is the native religion of Tibet. Research is still ongoing.

Even though Buddhism was spread in many parts of the world, nowadays Tibet is the only country where we find both the so-called Thegpa Menpa,[82] the Lower or Lesser Vehicle, and the Greater Vehicle, including Tantra; Mahayana, Hinayana and Vajrayana, those three are only found together in Tibet. In Indian Buddhism, this Great Vehicle, the teachings of Mahayana, appeared thanks to Nagarjuna.[83]

---

[80] For reference see footnote 29, page 5.

[81] Tib. ban de / བན་དེ།

[82] Tib. theg pa dman pa / ཐེག་པ་དམན་པ།

[83] Nagarjuna is said to have discovered the Prajñāpāramitā Sutras, the foundation of Buddhist Mahayana traditions in India and elsewhere.

Nowadays, extreme sectarian views are generally a thing of the past and real, authentic discussion and research is underway. H.H. the XIV Dalai Lama holds that all religions are friends or should have friendly relationships, so he is organizing meetings and discussions and recognizing that the basis of all religions is compassion and loving kindness. He says there is no reason why there should be conflict.

Q: First of all, I would like to make it clear that I want to become a Buddha. But I am wondering about what the effect is when I or anyone else becomes a new Buddha. Is there any extra benefit or extra activity in addition to the activities already being accomplished by the existing Buddhas? From the sentient beings' side, is there any extra benefit for even one single sentient being if I or someone else becomes a new Buddha, and from the Buddhas' side, is their activity expanding or changing in some way?

A: So now we are in the twenty-first century. In the twenty-first century there is the idea that the tradition should be modernized and each lama is doing his own way to combine the tradition with the ideas of our modern times. But as regards the Buddhas, they have absolutely no obscurations. It is said that the *bodhisattvas* have only one of the two types of obscurations[84] while the Buddhas have none, thus having no obscuration whatsoever they have no idea of: 'Let me gather

---

[84] Two Obscurations Tib. sgrib pa gnyis / སྒྲིབ་པ་གཉིས། are Emotional Obscurations Tib. nyon sgrib / ཉོན་སྒྲིབ། which are the opposites of the Ten Paramitas; and Cognitive Obscurations (or Obscurations of Knowledge) Tib. shes sgrib / ཤེས་སྒྲིབ། which have two aspects: Imputational Obscurations Tib. kun btags / ཀུན་བཏགས། and Coemergent Obscurations Tib. lhan skyes / ལྷན་སྐྱེས། Even High Bodhisattvas still have some subtle Coemergent Obscurations which are finally purified at the very end of the Fourth Path, the Path of Meditation Tib. sgom lam / སྒོམ་ལམ། after which a Bodhisattva enters the Fifth Path, The Path of No More Learning Tib. mi slob pa'i lam / མི་སློབ་པའི་ལམ། which is Buddhahood. On Five Paths see: Namdak, Yongdzin Lopön Tenzin. The Nine Ways of Bön; A Compilation of Teachings in France, Volume I, 9 September – 9 December 2006, BÖN OF FRUIT, Trnscr. & ed. Carol Ermakova and Dmitry Ermakov (Blou: Shenten Dargye Ling, 2006), pp.126-127.

students and teach them my own way.' They simply spontaneously accomplish whatever is to be done without any conceptual intention. Whatever is necessary to tame beings, this the Buddhas accomplish.

Monks and lamas should study science. We are doing this! American scientists come and they teach in the monasteries. They come. The monks study science nowadays. One monk has gone to America now. He has been studying science. He got a scholarship from a university. He studied science for three years and he passed the exam. Don't worry – we are doing these things! The fact that the monks and lamas are studying science is an illustration of the fact that the Buddhas and *bodhisattvas* do whatever is proper to benefit sentient beings. In Menri monastery there are four monks who are studying modern science; I don't know about Triten Norbutse monastery. But let us first obtain Buddhahood, and then we shall see what to do for the sake of sentient beings. It will come naturally!

We have finished the explanation of the *ngöndro* or Preliminary Practices, of which Refuge and Bodhichitta are the main two. For someone who has already completed the full Preliminary Practices, it is a good thing – in fact it is necessary – to keep doing these practices in an uninterrupted way, to recite them twice a day, for example. As for those who have not yet done the Preliminary Practices, it is essential they do them fully.

Introduction to the Natural State

There are a few words of introduction by Gongdzo Ritröpa Chenpo[85] who said that in order to achieve Enlightenment one must first meditate. In order to meditate so that we can achieve Buddhahood, we

---

[85] Tib. Rme'u dDgongs mdzod Ri khrod chen po / རྨེའུ་དགོངས་མཛོད་རི་ཁྲོད་ཆེན་པོ། (1036 – 1096), founder of Athri Dzogchen Tib. A khrid Rdzogs chen / ཨ་ཁྲིད་རྫོགས་ ཆེན།.

must realize the View. In order to recognize or realize the View, we must be introduced to it via the Mengag,[86] the Pith Instructions. One should not be content to be merely introduced to it; one should also practise it. One should not be satisfied by merely practising it; one should manifest the experience of one's Natural State in one's own mind. One should not be satisfied by merely manifesting it; one should obtain the 'signs of heat,' the signs of realization. One should not be satisfied by merely obtaining the signs of realization; one should really accomplish the Fruit. One should not be content by merely accomplishing the Fruit; one should also accomplish vast activities for the sake of all beings.

Three Stages of Introduction

1. All appearances are mind

As regards the introduction, there are three stages. The first is the introduction to appearances as being our own mind. There is nothing which is not the mind; everything is merely the miraculous display of the mind. One should meditate upon all appearances being the display of the pure and perfect mind. For one who has realized that the mind is as the *yidam* and *mandala*-palace, all outer appearances are also realized as being the deity and *mandala*-palace. The one who has obtained mastery over his own mind has also obtained mastery over all outer appearances. The one who has gained such mastery can then transform any outer appearance into gold; they can transform all the earth into gold and all fire into water.

When one does not realize one's own Nature of Mind then when, for instance, the mind remains inside a hell being, all appearances appear as hell. In a similar way, when one is reborn as a hungry ghost, it means that our mind is inside a hungry ghost. In that case, for that being, all appearances appear as the hungry ghost realm.

---

[86] Tib. man ngag / མན་ངག

This applies to the beings of each of the Six Realms. In each realm, the beings have karmic traces which correspond to this type of rebirth, hence all appearances appear accordingly. When your mind becomes deluded, everything begins to appear in completely the wrong way, as in the dream or in the *bardo*.[87] Even some medicines or foods can be dubbed poison or undesirable.

It is different when the sense consciousnesses – not the mind – are deluded. Then we can have so-called hallucinations when we see a double moon or see a conch shell as being yellow, or a rope as a snake. Or it seems that trees are moving. When you sit in a car, for instance, and are driving along, it looks as though all the trees are moving. This means that our sense consciousness is deluded.

So there are two different cases: deluded mental consciousness or deluded sense consciousness. There is a slight difference but anyway, there are no appearances which are beyond the mind itself. Why is this? It is because there is no perceiver, no thinker whatsoever apart from the Primordial Wisdom of our own Awareness. Why so? Because it is not the appearances that make us think or which somehow actively appear to us in some way or other. Rather, it is our consciousness which goes towards appearances and grasps them. So then we can say that from beginningless time our mind has been influenced by ignorance, and, under the power of influence, we have always been grasping at 'self' and perceiving things in a completely deluded way; in this way, *rigpa* has been deluded. So then we should wake up from the deep sleep of the ignorance of delusion which is

---

[87] Tib. bar do / བར་དོ། means 'intermediary state.' There are six kinds of *bardo*: Bardo of Natural Abiding – what we call life; Bardo of Dream; Bardo of Meditation; Bardo of the Time of Death; Bardo of Primordial Bönku; Bardo of the Clear Light of Emptiness; Bardo of Taking Rebirth. For more, see Ermakov, Dmitry. *Bø and Bön: Ancient Shamanic Traditions of Siberia and Tibet in their Relation to the Teachings of a Central Asian Buddha*, (Kathmandu: Vajra Publications, 2008), pp. 574-581.

like a dream or a hallucination. In that way, everything appears as delusion which is not true. What we see is not true. All this phenomenal existence which is devoid of root or base can appear in whatever way we perceive it. For example, beings from each of the Six Realms perceive a bowl of water in six different ways.[88]

Finally, without going into too much detail, the text says that we must attain certainty that everything is only the mind, that everything is gathered back into the mind, that all these deluded appearances should be brought back to the mind and be done with. We must determine, firmly and clearly, that all deluded appearances are merely the mind.

2. What is the mind?

Now in the text there is a series of questions about the mind. This very mind which perceives the mind, how is it? Does it exist or not? If it exists, does it have a shape? A form? A colour? A size? A location? Is it long or short? We should check whether this mind actually exists or not, and if it does, then in what way.

As for its size, there is no measure of it being great or small. Nobody is able to show it. It has never been either seen by the eye or heard by the ear. It has no smell for the nose or taste for the tongue. It has never been perceived in any way. If it were an object, it would be possible for one to perceive it in some way.

If you check logically whether the mind exists or not, then if we suppose it exists, we must check whether it exists as colour, as shape and so on. But in fact we cannot find anything. So if we cannot find or identify this so-called mind, then is it in fact non-existent? So then you might suppose it is non-existent, yet still there is something

---

[88] I.e. hell-beings perceive water as molten metal or ice, hungry ghosts see it as pus, animals see it as their living environment (fish and marine animals) or something drinkable, humans see water as water, demi-gods see it as battlefield, and gods see it as nectar.

which makes us speak and think. Even what is going on right now in each of us – what is that?

The text says it appears unceasingly; you cannot deny it is there. We can ask ourselves whether perhaps this mind is completely devoid of existence but in fact there is something there; if we check well, there is something which experiences and there is also a base for speaking of Buddhas or sentient beings, of pure or impure karma or actions. There is definitely something, some cognizer is there. Yet this 'something' is utterly indefinable; it cannot be determined precisely. Nevertheless, its qualities are spontaneously perfected. It manifests in all sorts of various forms. Its nature is unborn yet it arises unceasingly. It is non-dual and cannot be formulated or expressed in any possible way, nor can it be grasped by thoughts. Its nature is completely transparent and cannot be thought of in any possible way. You can trust. You can trust something, can't you? If there is nothing, you cannot trust! If there is something, there may still be a doubt, but once you prove it, then you can trust, it is not difficult. This is very complicated.

I said your mind exists and I said it doesn't. It has no colour, no shape, no anything. Always 'no.' So then you can say there is nothing. That is true. 'So there is nothing, yes?' 'No!' Then it starts again. 'Aha, so there is something!' but can you trust it or not? Once you have explained it, you have to trust. You have to trust each other. You have to trust your Guru's teachings and what he said. All these things we are talking about relate to the movement of *sem*.[89] You have *sem* and *semnyi*[90] and you can trust *semnyi* is not *sem*. The text calls this Nature of Mind, the Self-Born Primordial Awareness and the King of Awareness – that is *semnyi*.

---

[89] Tib. sems / སེམས། – mind.
[90] Tib. sems nyid / སེམས་ཉིད། – Nature of Mind.

Then comes the question: so what is it actually that we call Buddha? What does Buddha look like? Then you have to ask: How can we see Buddha? Before we said there is no shape, no colour, but now we have to prove there is something, so what does it look like? No colour, no shape – what does it look like? We have to prove this! Now maybe it would be better if Khen Rinpoche explains…

The text goes on posing questions: So, this so-called Self-Arising Primordial Awareness, this King of Intrinsic Awareness, this so-called Buddha – where is it? Where does it abide? What does it consist of? What is it made of? When will we meet it? What does it look like?

Then comes the answer: Buddha is this very Awareness or consciousness which is not modified or corrupted by conceptual thought or artificial constructions or by following after the six sense consciousnesses. It is this. The text points it out in this way.

It is *rangsal*[91] – it shows itself clearly to itself. It is that which is clear in and by itself without any grasping, utterly clear and transparent. It is very famous! This very famous thing is just that. It is very popular. This is the very thing which we are trying to meditate upon until we make a hole in our bottom! This is the very thing which, though we speak of it a hundred times, it is still this. Even if we think about it a thousand times, it is none other than this. No matter how many questions you ask, we have not much to answer. There is no answer but this. That very thing which is beyond answers – that is it.

3. Where does the Natural State abide?
As for where it abides, it abides within oneself. And if you were to look for it elsewhere, even if you searched for thousands of years or eons, you still would not find it. Even if you searched for it for three

---

[91] Tib. rang gsal / རང་གསལ།

thousand eons, you would not find it. Where are such things mentioned? They are mentioned in Dzogchen texts.

The Natural State is there from the highest, Kuntu Zangpo, down to the smallest insect such as an ant. There is no question of size, of large or small, of good or bad, of higher or lower; it is equally present in all. This is the very thing which remains clearly in the form of the Three Kayas,[92] within one's own body, within this very material body, in the centre of the heart. Secretly, it remains in the expanse of the *kunzhi*,[93] the Universal Base – that is the *dharmakaya*.[94] This Awareness, unmodified and devoid of any grasping, is the very *dharmakaya*. The luminous Awareness is *sambhogakaya*. The expressive energy is *nirmanakaya*.

This is the introduction to the Three Kayas. These Three Kayas are naturally abiding within oneself and they are allowed to appear – or will be directly perceived – at the time of travelling the path.

How to practise Dzogchen

This is the introduction, but it is difficult to realize it from mere words. Therefore, we should practise fixation on the letter A, for instance, and when we realize the object of fixation is empty, then the subject which was focussing on it is also realized as empty. Within this Emptiness we realize the nature of clarity and the non-duality of emptiness and clarity.

We must definitely meditate. This word 'meditating' actually means 'familiarizing yourself with' that with which you were not familiar. This meditation should become constant. We should always be meditating; that is what 'habit' means. Thus once we have acquired

---

[92] Tib. sku gsum / སྐུ་གསུམ།།

[93] Tib. kun gzhi / ཀུན་གཞི།

[94] Tib. bon sku / བོན་སྐུ།

the habit of meditation, in all the three times – when we eat, when we sleep, when we move – our mind should be well established in the Natural State. It is very important to meditate regularly.

Do you agree or not?

In the same way, if you become more familiar with this State, you can easily recognize and be aware of this Natural State of the Mind among the many thoughts which occur in day to day life, automatically, naturally. That is what we call *rigpai rangtsug sempa*[95] which literally means 'one is able to remain in the Natural State of *rigpa*.' Usually we talk about integration,[96] so even when we walk or eat or are performing any kind of activity, although generally people think it is impossible to remain in the state of *rigpa*, in fact it is possible.

This *rigpa* is perhaps difficult to focus upon because it is empty. But still, if we get used to it through our meditation then we will very easily be able to settle into it and be able to integrate everything within this experience of Awareness. If we were to say it did not exist, that would not be the case. It does exist. But once we have said it exists, we have to say how it exists, we have to prove it. The way to prove it is through your meditation. When you do more meditation you will see how it exists. But if you try to explain the way in which it exists, then it goes beyond its existence – something like that. And it pervades all beings equally, from highest Kuntu Zangpo down to even the smallest insect. There is no differentiation between any size or thickness. It exists, and it pervades every sentient being, every living being.

The past has passed. The future is coming. The past is gone, the future has not come. Between there, there is the present. You have to stay in the present. Your mind is resting, watching. Resting is

---

[95] Tib. rig pa'i rang tshugs sems dpa' / རིག་པའི་རང་ཚུགས་སེམས་དཔའ།
[96] Tib. bsre ba / བསྲེ་བ།

better. Do not think anything. Then you will understand nothingness. There is nothing. You will be able to see what nothingness is. You can see what emptiness is. You can learn these things. But you have to go very slowly. The Preliminary Practices are the important thing. You have to practise these well, and then you can see something; there is value in this. You don't see it with your eye, there is no colour. But it has value. You can feel that something is a little different.

You will understand all this slowly, slowly thanks to the teachings of your Masters Yongdzin Rinpoche and Khenpo Rinpoche.

Yes, they will introduce you. Slowly, step by step. You will be able to understand these nonsense things one day.[97] You will just be doing something, working, reading or something, and then, suddenly: 'Oh! This is easy! Why was it so difficult to understand until now?' You will tell yourself this one day: 'How nice! Aha!' – It will come.

Questions and Answers

Q: Before we start again, could we just sit quietly for a few minutes together?

A: That is a good idea. How long shall we sit for – five minutes? Ten minutes? That is good. You should not follow the past. So let us meditate, and during this short session, please do not remember the thoughts of the past; the past is gone, it is no longer there, it does not exist anymore. Do not go forwards to the future; do not go in the direction of the future for the future does not exist, it is not there. Just remain. Just keep your *rigpa* or Awareness in the present instant. Let

---

[97] In Tibetan there are all sorts of phrases to try and explain this, but they are obscure and bizarre and extremely difficult to translate, so that is what His Holiness is referring to when he says 'nonsense.' The words are very strange and seem contradictory, but we will be able to understand everything slowly through being introduced and practising.

us chant the Guru Yoga prayer once and then remain in the Natural State. Do not waver from Intrinsic Awareness.

[Meditation]

We have a saying: just as you need a mirror to see your own face, so in the same way you need a lama to see the Nature of your own mind. The lama is a mirror. If the mirror is clean, you can see very clearly. But there are different lamas. Some lamas are very clever – they introduce you to the Nature of your own Mind very easily. Some lamas tell you too much and make you crazy! That is what it looks like. We don't mean anything bad. But it depends. Some lamas are good speakers, some are not good speakers. Some look nice, others don't. For some, if you see your Master, you can say: 'Oh! I have understood now!' Sometimes it is very easy. Sometimes it is difficult – you are learning and learning from a Master but you cannot understand! Then you have to tell the truth. Then it is easy. We have been saying these things. From the beginning we were teaching this. We have introduced you already, but it is still difficult. You are always thinking that you want to know another point, something special, something above or beyond. No. It is with you always. It is with us. What can I say!?

Sometimes it may happen that we get very angry or we get puffed up with pride, but at that very moment we should wonder: who is this one who is angry? Who is this one who is proud? When we turn our mind inwards, both the one who is proud and the pride itself sort of vanish. Pride is when you feel very strongly that you are right and you disregard the other's position – that is how conflicts appear.

Sometimes someone goes to court and is very, very angry. He wants to decide who is right or wrong. He says: 'I am right, I did this and that.' But at that time, you have to think: who is doing that? All these things are very strange, very serious, yet if you always face inwards, you can see yourself, and then you can understand. We say that this is something which happens on the outside – fighting and so many other things – but you have to think yourself, look inside yourself. Then you can understand.

Where does this anger come from? Where does it stay? Where does it disappear to? Think about these things. The mind is like the weather this morning, very clear, but then a cloud comes from space. Space is clear, but a cloud comes in space, stays in space and disappears in space. Anger comes from your Nature of Mind, stays in your Nature of Mind and disappears in your Nature of Mind. Do you agree or not? Please think over this by yourself again and again.

Final Advice

Now, to summarize, the main thing is, please, do not forget the objects of Refuge. Please, never forget to take Refuge. When you wake up in the morning, for example, your first thought should be that of taking Refuge, and then generating a good heart, or *bodhichitta*. I am aware that most of us have to work very hard. Some of us may have to do a lot of business or read a lot of things, but even though we are extremely busy, we can still take Refuge and generate good heart in the morning when we wake up or in the evening when we go to bed. We can also try to recognize our own Nature. With these three things we will slowly gain some stability. Also, when we are confronted by difficulties we must be confident in the objects of Refuge and then we will gain some stability. Problems will occur; there is nobody who doesn't have problems. There is nobody who has no sufferings or obstacles. There are certainly obstacles, but then our trust in the objects of Refuge must be very firm and stable. We must take Refuge when problems arise and never change our mind, reject the Three Jewels or generate wrong views. We should not expect all our obstacles to stop immediately and forever; this may happen one day but it is not for right now. In the meantime, we should not generate wrong views but should remain firm and confident in the objects of Refuge, always.

There is no way for human beings not to have sufferings. We should not think that there are some lofty people who have more serious concerns or bigger problems while small people have small problems; it is not like this. Suffering is the same for every person whether you are responsible for a whole state or just have your own worries; suffering is always the same. No matter who you may be or what sufferings you may be facing, you should put your trust and confidence in the objects of Refuge and be very stable in that.

We should also pray and generate great aspirations. We should also meditate. We should not think: 'Oh, there are those lofty, scholarly, knowledgeable, rich people who are able to do great things while we have next to nothing and we cannot meditate.' This is not the case. Everybody can equally pray and make prayers of aspiration, and meditate. There is no question of social rank or anything like that.

We should always take Refuge. We should never forget the objects of Refuge. Then they will surely protect us, whoever we are.

Perseverance

When we are meditating, many things can happen, especially in our body. This is because the balance between the elements might be altered. When such things happen, we should not think: 'Oh, this is too difficult. It is too hard for me to meditate. I'll just drop it.' Please, don't think this way. Go on with your meditation. When we meditate, it sometimes gets difficult; meditation is not always peaceful and comfortable. So if it becomes too hard, we can sometimes have problems in our mind – sadness or maybe depression. At that time we don't feel like doing meditation and we think: 'Oh, I can't meditate.' Even if we do try to meditate, our meditation is not so successful. But at that time one shouldn't think: 'It's too hard. I can't do this. I want to drop meditation.' You should continue with your meditation. Or when you are very happy and in a good state, and your meditation seems to be very successful and very good, you can stay meditating as long as you want – at that time, too, you shouldn't keep on for too long, or that can create a certain kind of attachment to meditation, and later on this can turn into an obstacle. So therefore you always have to be a good judge of your meditation, of the duration and the time of your meditation.

Right conduct

Our conduct makes a big difference for the success of our meditation. Therefore, we also have to have right, good and decent judgement about our behaviour or conduct.

Normally in the teaching texts it explains what kind of conduct you should follow and what sort of behaviour you should avoid. Sometimes we are overly friendly and it looks as though it is tending towards flattery. Sometimes we are overly unfriendly. We also have to make right and decent judgement about these kinds of things. We as human beings have certain normal behaviour and we should keep this, naturally, normally.

We have natural human behaviour and we should always try to keep in that natural way of acting, behaving and talking. We should not overly modify our behaviour, either in the right way or in the wrong way.

We live in the twenty-first century and so we are always under pressure to follow the fashion, to be dressed in a certain way or to eat all sorts of strange things, but we should not allow ourselves to be influenced too much and should keep in the normal way – just normal. To put it simply, we should not be extreme in anything.

We should not have too many superstitions or preoccupations, we should be content with what we have and not think too much about useless things. We should try to develop a strong sense of contentment and be satisfied with what we have.

Why is this? Because the Nature of Mind is natural. Sometimes we are too jealous, sometimes we are too angry, and sometimes we are not angry or jealous at all! It is always different. But if there is a government rule, follow it; you have to do it. It is the rule. If you are without a TV in your house, maybe the government will ask: 'Why don't you want to keep a TV?' Then you are angry again. No, you shouldn't be. You should follow the rule and go and buy a TV! You should have a car, a very good car. The government says this and you have to buy it. This is not my rule! But you have to follow the government rules in a natural way.

But as for meditation, general meditation, you should develop all these things we have talked about. Always ask the Masters here. All the monks you see here have studied for fifteen years in order to understand Dzogchen. They have done this, they know.

Questions and Answers:

Q: What kind of influence does our practice have on the members of our family? In my family, for example, the more I practise the worse things become for the other family members such as my brothers, sisters and children. They are going mad. Maybe the cause is in me, in my practice?

A: This should not happen if one practises in a right or natural way. If you practise with natural behaviour then things will slowly, slowly improve. Your children and other family members are all free. If they are not interested, you don't need to talk to them too much about meditation and what you are doing. You should act normally and keep your meditation in a very natural, normal way.

They will come and follow you eventually. It looks as though they are becoming wild when you are meditating, but I don't think it is like this. If they want to play while you are meditating, let them play. They cannot meditate. You should not teach them meditation if they don't listen to you or follow you, nor should you get angry. OK? You are studying meditation, you are meditating, so let them play if they want. Afterwards, naturally, slowly, they will become interested. You cannot control them. You should not tell them: 'When I am meditating you shouldn't play, you shouldn't be noisy.' You shouldn't tell them this. Am I right? They are free. I think they will come and follow you, slowly. You have your own rules, the rules of the parent; then there is the government rule. You have to follow that one! Try. Pray: 'May they be good children!' Take Refuge for your family. This may be a help. We always pray that all sentient beings should find happiness and peace. Some beings, some people, are very wrathful but we still pray: 'Let them become peaceful and find peace.'

Q: Can you give us some advice as to how we can best support the spread of the teachings in this part of the world?

A: Mönlam,[98] prayer. That is precisely our aim when we gather here, for example. When we are gathered here and when together we make prayers and aspirations, it is said that these wishes have tremendous power. That is the very reason we are gathering here and saying these prayers all together. The purpose of gathering here is to receive teachings and to learn something. But this is not only of benefit to ourselves; it is of benefit to all sentient beings and for peace in the whole world. Now Yongdzin Rinpoche and I are quite old, but the lamas here are young, and they are supporting us and we are helping them. In particular, here we have these young lamas and they stay here and give teachings, so you can benefit from these teachings and you can also help and support the lamas and the centre, so everyone can

---

[98] Tib. smon lam / སྨོན་ལམ།

work together and support each other. As a result, there will be peace and happiness in the world, and in each and every individual because we are all working towards this; the aim of all activities is benefit, happiness and peace for each sentient being.

It is really for this reason that we are making prayers of aspiration, and one should not think that there are the 'good' prayers of the 'lofty' people and the worthless prayers of the low, mediocre people; we should all say all these prayers. It was the old tradition to make prayers of aspiration in the morning, at noon, in the evening – basically, all the time. Especially when we gather here, we gather to receive teachings and so on, and we are very fortunate, we have the lamas here and we receive good teachings, so we should really make prayers of aspiration for the sake of all beings.

So let us now pray such a prayer: 'May all the infinite sentient beings who have been our mothers in lives past reach full and perfect enlightenment! May they all be happy and at ease! May they all be free from suffering!' Let us make such a prayer of aspiration.

Bibliography

Bru-sgom rGyal-ba g.yung-drung, tr. Kvaerne, Per & Thubten K. Rikey, *The Stages of A-Khrid meditation: Dzogchen Practice of the Bon Tradition*, (Dharamasala: LTWA, 1996).

Ermakov, Dmitry. *Bə and Bön: Ancient Shamanic Traditions of Siberia and Tibet in their Relation to the Teachings of a Central Asian Buddha*, (Kathmandu: Vajra Publications, 2008).

Geshe Gelek Jinpa, Trnscr. & Ed. Carol Ermakova, Dmitry Ermakov. *Tummo: A Practice Manual by Shardza Tashi Gyaltsen*, (Blou: Shenten Dargye Ling, 2006).

Namdak, Yongdzin Lopön Tenzin. *Nine Ways of Bön; A Compilation of Teachings in France, Volume II, GENYEN THEGPA* (Blou: Shenten Dargye Ling, 2008).

Samten Chhosphel, *Exposition of the Nine Vehicles (According to the Nyingma and Bon Traditions*, Miscellaneous Series – 21, Bsam gtan chos phel, *Gsang sngags rnying ma dang g.yung drung bon gyi lugs gnyis las byung ba'i theg rim pa dgu'i rnam bzhag*, (Sarnath, Varanasi: Central Institute of Higher Tibetan Studies: 2006).

Yiltön Khyunggötsal. Transl. Yongdzin Lopön Tenzin Namdak, Trnscr. & Ed. Dmitry Ermakov, Carol Ermakova. *The Secret Practice of Khöpung Drenpa's Innermost Essence*, (Low Bishopley: FPYB, 2013).

Suggested Reading

Gyaltsen, Shardza Tashi. Commentary by Lopon Tenzin Namdak, *Heart Drops of Dharmakaya: Dzogchen Practice of the Bön Tradition* (Ithaca: Snow Lion Publications, 1993).

Karmay, Samten G. *The Treasury of Good Sayings* (Delhi: Motilal Banarsidass Publishers Private Limited, 1972).

Latri Nyima Dagpa, *Opening the Door to Bön*, (Ithaca, New York, Boulder, Colorado: Snow Lion, 2005).

Namdak, Yongdzin Lopön Tenzin. Trnscr. & ed. Ermakova, C. & Ermakov, D. *Masters of the Zhang Zhung Nyengyud: Pith Instructions from the Experiential Transmission of Bönpo Dzogchen*, (New Delhi: Heritage Publishers, 2010).

_____. Transl., trnscr. & ed. Nagru Geshe Gelek Jinpa, Ermakova, C. & Ermakov, D. *The Heart Essence of the Khandro, Experiential Instructions on Bönpo Dzogchen: Thirty Signs and Meanings from Women Lineage-Holders*, New Delhi: Heritage Publishers, 2012

_____. Trnscr. & ed. John Myrdhin Reynolds, *Bonpo Dzogchen Teachings*, (Kathmandu: Vajra Publications, 2006).

Reynolds, John Myrdhin. *The Oral tradition of Zhang-Zhung: An Introduction to the Bonpo Dzogchen Teachings of the Oral Tradition from Zhang-Zhung know as the Zhang-zhung snyan-rgyud* (Kathmandu: Vajra Publications, 2005).

Tr. Sangye Tanbar, Ed. Richard Guard. *The Twelve Deeds: A brief Life Story of Tonpa Shenrab, the founder of the Bon religion*, (Dharamasala: LTWA, 1995).

Snellgrove, David. *The Nine Ways of Bön*, (London: Oxford University Press, 1967).

Contents

9 780995 536807